THIS COLORING BOOK

belongs to...............

Farting cats coloring book

Farting cats coloring book

Farting cats coloring book

Farting cats coloring book

4

Farting cats coloring book

5

Farting cats coloring book

Farting cats coloring book

7

Farting cats coloring book

Farting cats coloring book

Farting cats coloring book

Farting cats coloring book

Farting cats coloring book

12

Farting cats coloring book

13

Farting cats coloring book

14

Farting cats coloring book

15

Farting cats coloring book

16

Farting cats coloring book

17

Farting cats coloring book

18

Farting cats coloring book

19

Farting cats coloring book

Farting cats coloring book

21

Farting cats coloring book

22

Farting cats coloring book

23

Farting cats coloring book

24

Farting cats coloring book

25

Farting cats coloring book

26

Farting cats coloring book

27

Farting cats coloring book

28

Farting cats coloring book

29

Farting cats coloring book

30

Farting cats coloring book

31

Farting cats coloring book

32

Farting cats coloring book

33

Farting cats coloring book

34

Farting cats coloring book

35

Farting cats coloring book

36

Farting cats coloring book

37

Farting cats coloring book

38

Farting cats coloring book

39

Farting cats coloring book

40

Farting cats coloring book

THANK YOU FOR CHOOSING MY COLORING BOOK.
IF YOU LIKE IT, I WOULD GREATLY APPRECIATE IF
YOU COULD LEAVE YOUR REVIEW ON AMAZON.
THIS MEANS SOOO MUCH TO ME

IF YOU WANT TO SEE MORE OF MY
OTHER COLORING BOOKS FOR KIDS,
PLEASE VISIT MY AUTHOR PAGE.
JUST **SCAN THE QR CODE** BELOW.

Farting cats coloring book

Made in United States
Troutdale, OR
11/20/2023

14780438R00051